# Matthew Henson

## Maryann N. Weidt

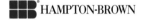 HAMPTON-BROWN

THE EXCHANGE

Is it necessary
to have goals?
Why or why not?

*To Jack, my little explorer*

Map on p15 by Laura Westlund
Illustrations by Tim Parlin

*Matthew Henson* by Maryann N. Weidt. Text copyright 2003 by Maryann N. Weidt.
Published by arrangement with Lerner Publications Company, a division of Lerner
Publishing Group. All rights reserved.

Introductions, questions, on-page glossaries, The Exchange © Hampton-Brown.

Hampton-Brown
P.O. Box 223220
Carmel, California 93922
800-333-3510
www.hampton-brown.com

Printed in the United States of America

ISBN 0-7362-2796-2

05 06 07 08 09 10 11 12 13 14 10 9 8 7 6 5 4 3 2 1

# TABLE OF CONTENTS

# INTRODUCTION

**M**atthew Henson was the first African American to travel to the North Pole, the top of the world. He lived during a time when most African Americans struggled just to **make a living**. Very few had a chance to **make a mark on history**. Matt spent many years **exploring the frozen Arctic** with Robert Peary. Matt tried and failed to reach the Pole many times, but he never gave up his dream. By showing great strength and courage, he proved that a black man could be an American hero.

This is his story.

........................................................................................

**make a living** earn enough money for themselves and their families

**make a mark on history** do something so important that people tell about it in history books

**exploring the frozen Arctic** going to a very cold area of the world

*Matthew Henson has a hard life.*
*He has to work hard just to eat. But his dream is*
*to travel around the world.*

# 1 IN SEARCH OF ADVENTURE

**M**atthew Alexander Henson was born in a cabin in Charles County, Maryland, on August 8, 1866. The **Civil War** had ended just a year earlier. **Slavery had been outlawed**, so African Americans were going through a time of great change.

....................................................................

**Civil War**  war between the Northern and Southern United States

**Slavery had been outlawed**  People could not own African Americans as slaves anymore

**To pay rent, sharecroppers gave their landlord a share of the crops they grew.**

Life wasn't easy for the Henson family. Matt's parents had never been slaves, but they still lived a hard life. They worked as sharecroppers, renting farmland owned by a white man. They were very poor. Finally, Matt's family moved to Washington, D.C., hoping to find a better life.

Sadly, Matt's life became even harder. When he was seven, his mother died. His father **couldn't afford** to take care of him, so Matt went to live with his uncle. Then his father died, too. **To make matters worse**, when Matt was thirteen his uncle told him he could no longer afford to take care of him.

.........................................................................................

**couldn't afford** did not have enough money
**To make matters worse** To add to the bad things

Matt **was forced to** find a job. He found work washing dishes at a restaurant. Matt worked hard and learned fast. Soon, he was cooking and waiting on tables, too. But he was bored. He knew he didn't want to spend his whole life doing restaurant work.

At least Matt enjoyed the people he met at the restaurant. A sailor named Baltimore Jack often ate there. Matt loved to hear Jack's stories of **life at sea**. Sailing around the world sounded exciting—much more exciting than working in a restaurant. Matt decided to quit his job and become a sailor.

**Matt spent much of his childhood in Washington, D.C. He lived in one of the poorest parts of the city.**

---

**was forced to** had to; would have nothing to eat if he did not

**life at sea** a sailor's life

**BEFORE YOU MOVE ON...**

1. **Details** Why was life hard for Matt when he was a child?

2. **Inference** Reread page 8. What kind of person was Matthew?

**LOOK AHEAD** Read pages 9–13 to find out if Matt finds the exciting job he wants.

In Matt's time, many young men looked for adventure as sailors on trading ships.

One of the biggest **shipping ports** in the country was in Baltimore, forty miles north of Washington, D.C. Matt figured he could **sign on** with a ship there. He hiked all the way there and walked straight to the **docks**. Tall ships floated in the harbor. Matt stared in awe at a big ship with three masts. The golden letters of the ship's name sparkled in the sunlight: *Katie Hines*.

The commander of this fine ship was Captain Childs. Matt told the captain that he wanted to be a sailor. Captain Childs admired the courage that Matt had shown by hiking all the way from Washington, D.C. He offered Matt a job.

............................................................................................

**shipping ports**  places where ships come and go
**sign on**  get a job
**docks**  places where ships park

Matt learned to use tools like these, which helped sailors guide their ships across the globe.

For the next five years, Matt worked hard for Captain Childs. He became a fine sailor. The captain **took a liking to** the eager young man. **He treated Matt like a son** and shared his books with him.

With Captain Childs, Matt traveled to some of the faraway places he was reading about. He saw Spain, France, Russia, Japan, Jamaica, and the Philippines.

Matt enjoyed his life as a sailor. But when he was eighteen, Captain Childs died. Matt was alone once again. He **lost interest in** ships and traveling and decided to look for work in the United States.

..........................................................................................

**took a liking to** liked

**He treated Matt like a son** He was nice to Matt like he would be to a son

**lost interest in** did not care about

Robert Peary grew up in Maine and spent much of his childhood camping and hiking.

Matt was a strong, smart, hardworking young man. But he still had a hard time finding a good job because of the color of his skin. Good jobs went to white people. Most African Americans had to do difficult and dirty work that paid little money.

Matt moved back to Washington, D.C. There he found work **stocking shelves** in a clothing store called B. H. Steinmetz and Sons.

One day, a man named Robert Peary walked into the store to buy some clothes for a trip. The United States government had asked him to explore Nicaragua, a country in Central America.

..................................................................................

**stocking shelves**  putting things on shelves

Along with new clothes, Robert needed a servant to help him on his journey. He could see that Matt was big and strong. After talking to him, Robert realized that Matt was smart, too. Mr. Steinmetz had already told Robert that Matt was a hard worker.

## CANAL QUEST

The U.S. government sent Robert to Nicaragua to see if a canal–a human-made **waterway**–could be built there. The canal would allow ships to pass through the country, linking the Atlantic and Pacific Oceans. At that time, ships traveling between the two oceans had to sail all the way around Cape Horn–the **southern tip** of South America. Building a canal through Central America would make the trip much faster. **Eventually**, a canal was built in Panama instead of Nicaragua. It is called the Panama Canal.

**waterway** place where water can pass
**southern tip** piece of land that is the farthest south
**Eventually** Later

That was all Robert needed to know. He asked Matt to be his servant on the trip to Nicaragua. Although Matt **wasn't thrilled** about working as a servant, he **jumped at the chance for** a new adventure.

Matt sailed to Nicaragua with Robert in November 1887 at the age of twenty-one. As Robert's servant, Matt did simple chores like cleaning Robert's clothes. But soon he was helping Robert to study the land, too.

Every night, Matt fell asleep to the sound of monkeys howling and alligators splashing. Matt liked his life as an explorer. He realized he wanted to do more with his life than work in a clothing store.

**Matt and Robert in Nicaragua in 1888**

----

**wasn't thrilled** was not excited

**jumped at the chance for** really wanted to go on

**BEFORE YOU MOVE ON...**

1. **Comparisons** How was Matt's life on the ship different from what it was on land?

2. **Text Feature** How is "Canal Quest" on page 12 different from the rest of the text? How does it help you understand why Robert went to Nicaragua?

**LOOK AHEAD** Read pages 14–17 to find out why Matt and Robert go to Greenland.

*Matt and Robert travel to the far north.*
*They meet the Inuit people. They learn about survival*
*and also the dangers of the North.*

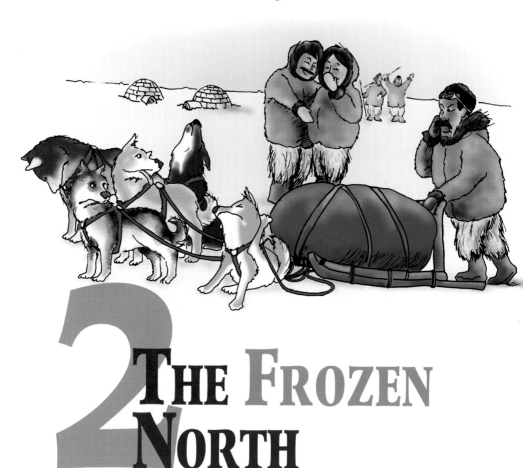

# 2 THE FROZEN NORTH

The exploration of Nicaragua lasted seven months. When Matt returned, he went back to work at Steinmetz's store. But he missed the excitement of living in a **strange** place. He also missed having a job that **challenged** him.

........................................................................

**strange** new and interesting

**challenged** was not boring for; was exciting to

**Greenland and the North Pole**

NORTH POLE

ARCTIC OCEAN

ICELAND

Ellesmere Island

G R E E N L A N D

RUSSIA

ARCTIC OCEAN

Ellesmere Island

GREENLAND

ICELAND

Alaska

CANADA

UNITED STATES

In 1891, Matt got his chance for a new adventure. Robert asked him to help explore the northern tip of Greenland. This huge island is in **the deadly cold Arctic**, the world's most northern region.

Robert was traveling to Greenland because he wanted to be the first person to reach the North Pole, the top of the world. He hoped that exploring Greenland would be a first step in finding a **route** to the Pole.

....................................................................................

**the deadly cold Arctic** an area of the world so cold that it is dangerous

**route** way for people to travel

# THE NORTH POLE

The North Pole isn't really a pole, like the kind you might find sticking out of the ground. It is the northernmost spot on the globe, the very top of the earth. When Matt began exploring the Arctic, the North Pole was one of the last places in the world that humans hadn't visited. Many adventurers **risked their lives** for the **honor of being the first** to reach the Pole.

Matt knew the trip would be dangerous. But it would also be exciting. On June 6, 1891, he **set sail** with Robert for Greenland. As the ship headed north, the weather grew colder. Looking out from the deck of the ship, Matt saw all sorts of amazing things. A walrus poked its head out of the icy water. Barking seals and giant polar bears perched on the ice. Matt stared at icebergs as big as houses.

---

**risked their lives**  knew that they might die
**honor of being the first**  respect of being the first person
**set sail**  left on a ship

When the ship reached Greenland, the explorers **set up camp**. They would stay through the winter, learn how to hunt and **survive** the cold, and then **journey** across the island in the spring.

The explorers weren't the only people living in the area. Native people lived there, too. They called themselves Inuit.

........................................................................................

**set up camp**  stopped to make places to sleep and cook outside

**survive**  stay alive in

**journey**  travel

The Inuit sometimes hunted polar bears for their meat and fur.

**BEFORE YOU MOVE ON...**

1. **Sequence** Reread page 15. Robert wanted to go to the North Pole, so why did he go to Greenland first?

2. **Summarize** Reread "The North Pole" on page 16. What is the North Pole?

**LOOK AHEAD** Read pages 18–21 to find out what it was like for Matt to meet the native people of Greenland.

**The Inuit lived in houses made of snow called igloos.**

Some of the Inuit people decided to live near the camp. Robert began trading with them. He exchanged things the Inuit could use, such as knives, guns, pots, and pans, for things the explorers needed—fur coats, pants, and mittens.

Matt **struck up friendships** with the Inuit. Although Robert **got along well** with them, Matt was the only explorer who learned to speak their language. After a hard day of work, Matt sat and shared jokes and stories with the Inuit late into the night.

The Inuit liked Matt, too. At first, they thought he was Inuit because he had dark skin like theirs.

....................................................................................

**struck up friendships** became friends
**got along well** was friendly

The Inuit taught Matt and the other explorers how to survive in the Arctic. They taught them to hunt reindeer and musk ox for their meat and fur. They also showed the explorers how to drive a sled with a team of Arctic dogs. The explorers would use the dogsleds to travel across Greenland's frozen, snow-covered ground.

At first, Matt's Inuit friends laughed at **his clumsy sled driving**. But he practiced until he became an expert.

**A group of Inuit with their sled dogs. Explorers such as Robert and Matt called the Inuit people Eskimos.**

........................................................................

**his clumsy sled driving** how hard it was for him to drive a sled

**Robert and the other explorers wore Arctic animal furs to fend off the icy cold.**

When spring came, Matt, Robert, and several other men set off to explore northern Greenland. Matt hadn't gone far when he ripped his boot on some **jagged** ice. Pain shot through his heel, and he **started to limp**.

Even though it was spring, the Arctic weather was still so cold that Matt's foot was in danger of freezing. A frozen foot would have to be cut off. Robert ordered Matt to go back to camp and let his foot **heal**. Matt obeyed, leaving Robert and the other men to explore northern Greenland.

........................................................................................

**jagged** sharp
**started to limp** could not walk well
**heal** get better

Months later, Matt, Robert, and the other explorers returned to the United States. Matt was disappointed that he had missed the most exciting part of the **expedition**. But on the voyage home, Robert told Matt he was already planning another trip. Matt would have another chance to explore the Arctic.

........................................................................................

**expedition** exploration trip

**Matt and one of his Inuit friends return from a hunting trip.**

**BEFORE YOU MOVE ON...**

1. **Inference** What was it about Matt that made the Inuit people like him?

2. **Summarize** Why was this trip to Greenland important for Robert and Matt?

**LOOK AHEAD** Read pages 22–25. Will Matt have another chance to get to the North Pole?

*Matt travels to the Arctic again and again.*
*But in between trips, his work is very different.*

# 3 TRY, TRY AGAIN

It turned out that Matt had many more chances to explore the Arctic. From 1893 to 1902, Matt and Robert made several more journeys to Greenland.

On the first trip, Matt, Robert, and their team of explorers **made their first attempt at reaching** the North Pole. They traveled as far as the northeast coast of Greenland, but steep cliffs **kept** them from going farther north.

On another journey, Matt, Robert, and their team of explorers took a different route. For the first time, they left land and traveled out onto the frozen Arctic Ocean. On the ocean, the explorers **ran up against** huge walls of ice called pressure ridges. Some were as tall as five-story buildings. These ridges were difficult to climb and made traveling slow.

**Pressure ridges were bumpy, steep, and slippery.**

---

**made their first attempt at reaching**  tried for the first time to go all the way to

**kept**  stopped

**ran up against**  had to find a way to walk or climb over

The explorers cross a narrow lead. Some leads were as wide as football fields.


**Large patches** of open water called leads also slowed them down. If a lead was **narrow**, Matt could chop a section of ice and use it as a **ferry** to cross the water. But crossing a lead was dangerous work. Matt knew that if he slipped and fell into the icy water, he would freeze to death in minutes.

During these journeys across the Arctic Ocean, Matt and Robert traveled to places that no one had ever visited before. But they did not reach the North Pole.

......................................................................

**Large patches** Big areas
**narrow** small
**ferry** boat

**Between journeys**, Matt returned to the United States. For Matt, life in the United States was very different from life in the Arctic. In the Arctic, the Inuit and Matt's fellow explorers **treated him with respect**. But in the United States, **he was often treated poorly** because of the color of his skin. He had a hard time finding a good job. Eventually he found work with the Pennsylvania Railroad. The job wasn't much fun, but Matt enjoyed traveling around the country.

......................................................................................

**Between journeys**  When he was not traveling

**treated him with respect**  were nice to him

**he was often treated poorly**  people were not nice to him

During the early 1900s, railroad work was one of the best-paying jobs a black man could have.

**BEFORE YOU MOVE ON...**

1. **Main Idea and Details**  Matt and Robert tried again and again to reach the North Pole. What stopped them?

2. **Comparisons**  Reread page 25. How was Matt's life in the United States different from his life in the Arctic?

**LOOK AHEAD**  Read pages 26–28 to find out about Matt's other love.

When Matt returned from the Arctic in 1902, he spent some of his time working for the railroad. He also helped Robert to prepare for their next trip.

During that time, he met and fell in love with a woman named Lucy Ross. He wanted to marry her. But Robert was planning to return to the Arctic. He wanted Matt to join him. Matt was happy to go, but he didn't want to leave Lucy. He asked Lucy to marry him when he returned. Lucy said yes.

## PULLMAN PORTER

Matt worked as a Pullman porter for the Pennsylvania Railroad. His job was to serve passengers traveling in Pullman cars—fancy railroad cars made for dining and sleeping. **His duties included** serving food to passengers and setting up their beds at night. For Matt, the best part of the job was seeing the United States. **His travels took him** to Ohio, Illinois, Minnesota, California, Florida, and many other states.

**His duties included** His work was
**His travels took him** He went

**Robert often said that Matt was one of the best sled dog drivers in the world.**

In 1905, Matt and Robert returned to the Arctic to **make another run for** the Pole. On this trip, Matt and Robert again traveled farther north than anyone had ever gone—within 174 miles of the Pole. But leads as wide as football fields made traveling difficult. Sometimes the explorers had to wait for days for the leads to **freeze up**. The delays took up so much time that the explorers **ran low on** food and supplies. Once again, they had to turn back.

..................................................................................

**make another run for**  try again to go all the way to
**freeze up**  become ice
**ran low on**  used almost all of their

Matt and Robert returned to the United States in late 1906. Matt and Lucy were married a few months later. They moved into an apartment in Harlem, New York. For the first time since he was thirteen years old, Matt finally had a home and someone to love.

Matt was happy with his life with Lucy, but **his desire to reach the Pole was still strong**. Robert told Matt he was going to make one more attempt to get there. Matt **agreed to** come along on the expedition. After so many years of trying and failing, he wanted to try one more time.

..................................................................................

**his desire to reach the Pole was still strong**  he really wanted to go to the Pole

**agreed to**  said he would

**BEFORE YOU MOVE ON...**

1. **Author's Purpose** Reread page 28. Why does the author write, "Matt finally had a home"?

2. **Details** Matt and Robert got 174 miles from the Pole. What problems stopped them?

**LOOK AHEAD** Read pages 29–32 to find out what makes the next trip so difficult.

*Matthew makes one more trip to the Arctic.*
*The explorers face some of the most dangerous*
*and difficult times on this trip.*

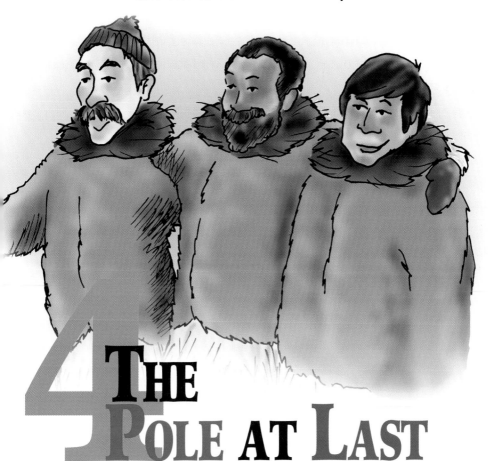

# 4 THE POLE AT LAST

On July 6, 1908, Matt, Robert, and their crew set sail for the Arctic. As Matt's ship sailed away from the steamy heat of New York City, he saw sheep **grazing** on green hills. Before long, Matt knew, he would see white polar bears **lumbering** across snow and ice.

........................................................................................

**grazing**  eating grass

**lumbering**  moving with heavy steps

When the ship reached the Arctic, a group of Inuit joined the expedition. On February 18, 1909, the group set off for the Pole. The journey was rough. **Viciously cold winds howled** in the explorers' faces. Matt's arms and legs ached as he pushed the sleds over **mounds** of snow and ice. Stuffed with more than five hundred pounds of supplies, each sled **made a heavy burden**.

**The pack ice that Matt and Robert traveled was bumpy and slippery. It seemed to go on forever.**

...................................................................................

**Viciously cold winds howled** Very strong, cold winds blew

**mounds** little hills

**made a heavy burden** was very hard to push

**Sometimes the only way to get past a pressure ridge was to chop through it with a pickax.**

Each day Matt and the other explorers raced across the frozen Arctic. Often they had to stop because huge pressure ridges blocked their path. To get through the ridges, Matt and the explorers had to chop through the frozen snow with pickaxes. It was hard work. The cold made Matt's fingers burn. The blowing snow felt like needles hitting his face. Even his nose, which normally did not get cold, **felt numb**. But Matt and the other explorers kept chopping.

...........................................................................................

**felt numb**   had no feeling when he touched it

As if pushing sleds all day wasn't enough, Matt and his team had to build a **snow igloo** at the end of each day. The explorers cut out blocks of snow with long knives. The men stacked the blocks to make the igloo. Then they filled in the cracks between the blocks with more snow to keep out the wind. Inside the igloo, they ate a dinner of frozen **beef jerky** and dried biscuits—not very tasty.

## SLED DOGS

Inuit sled dogs were big and strong, weighing eighty to one hundred pounds. They had thick, bushy fur that could keep them warm even when temperatures dropped to -50°F. Matt was amazed by how strong the dogs were, and how they could pull a heavy sled for hours without tiring. Although Matt liked the dogs, they weren't always friendly. They usually tried to bite him when he hooked them up to the **sled harness**.

**BEFORE YOU MOVE ON...**

**1. Viewing** What do the photographs on pages 30–31 tell you about the ice?

**2. Cause and Effect** Why were the sled dogs good for pulling sleds in the Arctic?

**LOOK AHEAD** Read pages 33–36 to find out if Matt's dream comes true.

**snow igloo** little house made of snow
**beef jerky** dried beef
**sled harness** ropes on the sled

**The bumpy ice was tough on sleds. Matt was an expert at repairing them.**

Some nights it was so cold—even inside the igloo—that Matt and the others woke up several times and **flapped** their arms and legs to warm up. Otherwise they might have frozen to death.

The explorers traveled on. Days and weeks passed. The temperature warmed up a little—to −8°F. With the warmer weather came open water and soft snow. The dogs and the sleds **got stuck** in the soft snow. Time after time, Matt had to lift them out. Then it was back to the jagged ice again.

.......................................................................................

**flapped**  quickly moved
**got stuck**  stopped many times

Matt, Robert, and the other explorers were **dead tired**, but they knew they were **getting close**. They **were determined not to give up**.

Late in the day on April 6, 1909, the explorers set up camp on the frozen Arctic ice. While Matt was building an igloo for the team to rest in, he watched Robert pull a package out of his coat. When Matt saw what the package was, he realized they had finally reached their goal.

**During the final days of the journey to the Pole, the explorers stopped to sleep for only a few hours a night.**

.......................................................................................

**dead tired**  very, very tired

**getting close**  very near to the North Pole

**were determined not to give up**  decided they definitely would not stop

Robert took this photo at the North Pole. Matt is in the center, holding the flag Robert had brought along on every one of their polar adventures.

In Robert's hand was a **ragged** old American flag. Many years ago, Robert had said he would **plant this flag** at the North Pole. Robert unfolded the flag and planted it on top of the igloo. Matt could hardly believe it. After eighteen years of trying and failing, there they were—at the top of the earth.

......................................................................................

**ragged** torn
**plant this flag** put the flag in the ground

"Hip, hip, hooray!" Matt shouted into the wind. He had achieved his goal, but the journey was only half over. They had to make it back to land. And they had to get there before the weather got too warm. Warm weather meant more open water. Without ice to travel on, they might be **stranded** on the ocean and die.

Matt, Robert, and the Inuit stayed at the North Pole for just one day before heading back to land. On the journey home, the team traveled far and fast. They slept only a few hours each night. They **covered** 485 miles in seventeen days and reached land on April 23.

Back at camp, Matt **peered** at the faces of the other men. They looked wrinkled and old. He looked at his own face in a mirror and saw that he looked the same.

......................................................................................

**stranded**  left alone
**covered**  traveled
**peered**  looked closely

**BEFORE YOU MOVE ON...**

1. **Conclusions** Reread pages 34–35. It was an important moment for Matt when Robert pulled out the package. Why?

2. **Cause and Effect** Reread page 36. What would happen if the explorers didn't leave the Pole quickly?

**LOOK AHEAD** Read pages 37–40 to find out how the explorers are welcomed home.

*Matt is not famous when he gets back from his adventure. Many years later, some people remember him.*

# 5 A QUIET HERO

**B**ack in the United States, newspapers **praised** Robert for discovering the North Pole. They **ignored** Matt's important **role** in the expedition, calling him "Peary's colored servant."

..................................................................................

**praised**  said good things about

**ignored**  did not say anything about

**role**  work

**The National Geographic Society** awarded Robert a special gold medal. Other explorers in Matt and Robert's party—white men—also received medals. These men had not even reached the Pole. Matt received nothing.

Not everyone ignored Matt. African Americans were proud of Matt's **accomplishments**. A group of them held a dinner in New York City to honor him. They gave Matt a gold watch and chain.

**The African American community of New York City showed their admiration for Matt by giving him a gold watch.**

......................................................................................

**The National Geographic Society** A group that explores and teaches people about the world

**accomplishments** good work and his courage

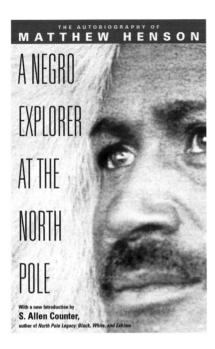

THE AUTOBIOGRAPHY OF
**MATTHEW HENSON**

A NEGRO
EXPLORER
AT THE
NORTH
POLE

With a new Introduction by
**S. Allen Counter,**
author of *North Pole Legacy: Black, White, and Eskimo*

**Lucy helped Matt write his book. She thought he deserved more attention for his work as an explorer.**

Matt was now forty-three years old, and his exploring days were over. He needed to earn a living for himself and Lucy. For a while, he gave speeches about his travels. But Matt didn't like talking to crowds. He said it was easier jumping across icy water than talking to a group of strangers.

Matt also wrote a book about his life as an explorer, *A Negro Explorer at the North Pole*. Robert wrote the introduction. He praised Matt's strength, intelligence, and "**determined heart**."

......................................................................

**determined heart** strong desire to succeed

Matt earned a small salary as a messenger for the United States government in New York City.

Despite his accomplishments, Matt still had a hard time finding a good job. After working for a while as a **parking garage attendant**, he finally became a messenger in New York City. The job didn't pay much, but it provided **steady work**. Matt **retired** at the age of seventy.

..................................................................

**parking garage attendant**  person who parks cars

**steady work**  work every day for many years

**retired**  stopped working

**BEFORE YOU MOVE ON...**

1. **Comparisons**  How were Robert and Matt treated differently when they got home? Why?

2. **Main Idea and Details**  How did Matt use what he learned from his trips?

**LOOK AHEAD**  Read about all the honors Matt finally received on pages 41–43.

Finally, in 1937, at the age of seventy-one, **Matt began to receive some attention** for his Arctic exploration. He was invited to join the New York Explorers Club. He was the club's first African American member. In 1946, the U.S. Navy honored Matt with a medal.

President Dwight D. Eisenhower invited Matt to the White House in 1954. The president praised Matt for his **contribution to** the discovery of the North Pole.

At the White House, Matt (far right) traces his travels on a globe. President Dwight D. Eisenhower (second from left) and Lucy (between them) listen to his story.

...................................................................................

**Matt began to receive some attention**  people began to talk about and remember Matt

**contribution to**  his important work in

Except for these awards and honors, Matt and Lucy lived a quiet life in Harlem, New York. Throughout the rest of his life, people would often stop Matt on the street to ask him about his Arctic adventures.

Matthew Henson died on March 9, 1955. He was eighty-eight years old. **His achievements** were not forgotten with his death. Thousands of people came to his funeral.

## GLORY AND HONOR

After his death, Matt received more and more honors. In 1959, Matt's home state of Maryland **proclaimed** April 6 Matthew Henson Day. (April 6 is the day Matt and Robert reached the North Pole.) In 1986, the United States Postal Service **issued** a stamp picturing Robert and Matt. A 1998 television movie called *Glory & Honor* showed Matt and Robert's struggle to reach the Pole. In 2000, the National Geographic Society honored Matt with a gold medal.

................................................................

**His achievements** The great things he did
**proclaimed** made
**issued** made

**Robert often said of Matt, "I can't get along without him."**

Many years after his death, Matt Henson is still a hero to many people. The Inuit still speak **fondly of** Matt. They recall his courage and **good humor**. A word Matt made up and often used—*ahdoolo*—has become part of the Inuit language. For the Inuit, the word means "someone who is brave of heart."

Matt Henson lived during a time when African Americans received little respect and had few choices about what to do with their lives. Matt had the courage and the rare chance to live a life of adventure. Through hard work and determination, he made his dream—and a dream of people everywhere—come true.

...................................................................................

**fondly of** nicely about
**good humor** cheerfulness

**BEFORE YOU MOVE ON...**

1. **Details** When did Matt become famous? What did people do to show that they thought he was a great man?

2. **Conclusions** Reread page 43. Why was Matthew Henson's life so important?

43

# Time Line

*In the year ...*

1873   Matt's mother died.

1879   his father died.
      he left his uncle's house to live on his own.    Age 13
      he got his first job.

1880   he joined the crew of the *Katie Hines.*

1887   he met Robert Peary.    Age 21
      he traveled to Nicaragua with Robert.

1891   he and Robert made their first journey to Greenland.
      he first met Inuit people.

1893   he set sail for the second journey to Greenland
      on June 26.

1898   he traveled to the Arctic and stayed for four years.

1902   he and Robert walked on the frozen Arctic Ocean
      for the first time.    Age 36

1905   he and Robert made another attempt to reach
      the Pole, but failed.

1907   he married Lucy Ross.    Age 41

1908   he set sail on the final attempt for the Pole.

1909   his team set out on the Arctic Ocean on March 1.
      he, Robert, and four Inuit reached the North Pole
      on April 6.

1912   he published *A Negro Explorer at the North Pole.*

1937   he was invited to join the New York Explorers Club.    Age 71

1954   President Eisenhower invited him to the White House.
                                                Age 88

1955   he died on March 9.

# A HERO'S BURIAL

When Matt died in 1955, he was buried in a **humble** grave near his home in New York City. Thirty-one years later, in 1986, a man named Dr. S. Allen Counter decided that a hero like Matt deserved to be buried alongside other American heroes. He wrote to President Ronald Reagan, asking that Matt be reburied in Arlington National Cemetery. The request was granted, and on April 6, 1988, Matt and his wife, Lucy, were reburied at Arlington–next to the graves of Robert Peary and his wife, Josephine. A bronze memorial was built **as a tribute to** Matt. The Hensons **now rest** in the same cemetery as American presidents, war heroes, explorers, and Supreme Court justices.

..................................................................................

**humble**  very simple, ordinary
**as a tribute to**  to honor
**now rest**  are buried

# FURTHER READING

Curlee, Lynn. *Into the Ice: the Story of Arctic Exploration*. **Boston: Houghton Mifflin Company, 1998.** Describes the Arctic ice cap and the expeditions that explored it.

Ferris, Jeri, *Arctic Explorer*. **Minneapolis, MN: Lerner Publications Company, 1989.** Read more about Matt's life and adventures. For older readers.

Henson, Matthew.  *A Negro Explorer at the North Pole*. **Montpelier, VT: Invisible Cities Press, 2001.** Matt's Arctic journey in his own words, in a new edition of the book he first published in 1912.

Johnson, Rebecca L. *A Walk in the Tundra*. **Minneapolis, MN: Carolrhoda Books, Inc., 2001.** Readers are led on a walk in the tundra, and learn about the plants and animals that live in this cold environment.

King, Wilma. *Children of the Emancipation*. **Minneapolis, MN: Carolrhoda Books, Inc., 2000.** Explores the lives of African American children in the late 1800s, when Matthew Henson was growing up.

Love, Ann, and Jane Drake. *The Kids Book of the Far North*. **Niagara Falls, NY: Kids Can Press Ltd., 2000.** Read about plant and animal life, ancient peoples, and everyday life in the Arctic environment.

Patent, Dorothy. *Polar Bears*. **Minneapolis, MN: Carolrhoda Books, Inc., 2000.** Learn more about the king of the Arctic and the biggest bear on earth.

# WEB SITES

**Matthew Henson Web Site**
**<http://www.matthewhenson.com/>** This site features photos
of Matt and his expeditions to the North Pole. It also includes
the titles of the latest books published about him.

**A Matthew Henson North Pole Museum**
**<http://www.matthewhenson.org/>** View photos of
Matt and his journeys, and listen to a recording of *Stealing the
Glory: The Conquest of the North Pole*, a story about Matt and
Robert Peary.

# SELECT BIBLIOGRAPHY

Counter, S. Allen. *North Pole Legacy: Black, White, and Eskimo.*
    Amherst, MA: The University of Massachusetts Press, 1991.

Dolan, Edward F. Jr. *Matthew Henson, Black Explorer.*
    New York: Dodd, Mead & Co., 1979.

Henson, Matthew A. *A Negro Explorer at the North Pole.*
    New York: Frederick A. Stokes Co., 1912.

Peary, Josephine. *My Arctic Journal.* New York:
    Contemporary Publishing Company, 1893.

Peary, Robert. *The North Pole.* New York: Stokes, 1910.

Robinson, Bradley. *Dark Companion.* New York: Robert M.
    McBride & Co., 1947.

# INDEX

**Acknowledgments**

**For photographs and artwork: Brown Brothers:** front cover, p4, p19, p20; **Collection of Bob Rathke:** p25; **CORBIS:** back cover (© Galen Rowell), p10 (© Tria Giovan), p17 (©John Conrad), p43 (© Bettman); **Dartmouth College Library:** p21, p27, p33, p34; **Dorothy H. Patent:** p.30; **Dwight D. Eisenhower Library:** p41; **Independent Picture Service:** p31, p38 (© Todd Strand); **Invisible Cities Press:** p39; **Library of Congress:** p9, p40; **MatthewHenson.com:** p45 (© Ron Williams); **National Archives:** p11, p23, p24, p35; **North Wind Picture Archives:** p7, p8, p18; **University of Michigan:** p13 (Hobbs Collection, Special Collections Library)

**For quoted material:** p. 39. Henson, Matthew A., *A Black Explorer at the North Pole.* New York: Walker and Company, 1969; p. 43, Dolan, Edward F., Jr., *Matthew Henson, Black Explorer.* New York: Dodd, Mead & Company, 1979.